ENERGY HEALING FOR PETS, WILDLIFE & SANCTUARY ANIMALS

ENERGY HEALING FOR PETS, WILDLIFE & SANCTUARY ANIMALS

How to Safely Offer Powerful and Effective Animal Healing

Marese Hickey

Animal Healer

Disclaimer

When your animal is sick, the first port of call is the vet. Energy healing is a very useful complementary therapy but is NOT a substitute for veterinary care. Please be sensible and bring your beloved pet to the vet (ordinary or holistic) if they are sick. Then supplement that treatment with energy healing to improve their ability to self-heal. It is not vet care OR energy healing - both are necessary and both can help.

This book and the methods outlined in it are not intended to be a substitute for the care of a qualified veterinary practitioner. The author is not responsible for any consequences incurred by those employing the practices of energy healing or remedies outlined in it. Any application of the practices of energy healing or remedies described is at the discretion of the reader and is his or her sole responsibility. The practices of energy healing or remedies described are not intended to be used for diagnosis or veterinary treatment.

About the Author

Marese Hickey has done aerobatics in a vintage Tiger Moth in New Zealand, meditated in Tibet, and has swum with wild dolphins in the Bahamas. She is an energy healer, holistic therapist and former nurse. She has worked as a clinical hypnotherapist for twenty years. Marese is an animal healer and a servant to four cats. She has been a volunteer animal healer with Dog's Aid animal sanctuary in Dublin, Ireland for the last ten years.

Also by Marese Hickey

Self-Publishing for Beginners

The Tale of Harry Three Paws

The Power of Inner Change for Outer Results EBook Series

Vol. 1 Letting Go of the Past

Vol. 2 Mind Direction

Vol. 3 Yes to Life

How to Love Yourself in Less than 50 Years

For Veron,
my best buddy in the Universe
with love and thanks.

CONTENTS

Introduction

I had already been a therapist for humans for many years when my cat Gannet got cancer, but I had not studied energy healing. It was squamous cell carcinoma, common in cats with white ears. I got one ear flap removed but the cancer then became evident on the second ear, although it wasn't as bad. She was fourteen at the time, and I wanted to explore complementary therapies for her as opposed to putting her through a second surgery. I brought her to a healer down the country who worked with animals. "How is it different from healing on humans?" I asked him. "It isn't," he said. "Healing is healing."

Gannet had never seen a dog in her sheltered life and this man worked on her in his kitchen, with his four dogs milling around. She sat on my knee, rigid with fear. She was feral, and it had taken two years before she let me pat her on the head. As the healing progressed, she began to relax despite her best efforts, and turned into a sort of furry jelly cat. I made another appointment for the following week. That night, my head was whirling with energy - clearly the healing had affected me too. When I went to bring her for the second appointment, she ran away and I simply could not catch her. I rang to cancel the appointment, to explain and apologise. "I'll just have to study this old healing lark myself," I said jokingly. "Here's the number of a great Reiki Master who lives close to you," he said. And that was how it started.

I went on to become a Reiki Master, Seichem Master, Magnified Healing practitioner, a spiritual healer and did a Diploma in Animal healing in the UK. I am a clinical hypnotherapist, past life regressionist and Tapas Acupressure Therapy practitioner. I am also a registered general and paediatric nurse. The reason I am listing my qualifications for working with humans in a book on energy healing for animals is that I often work with pet guardians as well as their animals, as they are a unit and therefore, what impacts one, impacts the other. So if you are ready to start healing, keep reading!

Chapter 1

What is Healing?

Everything in nature has the intrinsic ability to restore itself.
Denise Linn, Shaman

Your pet is chronically ill, traumatised or has been written off by the vet. You are at your wit's end, having tried everything. You have been to different vets, spent a fortune, and your beloved pet is still suffering. When conventional veterinary treatment is not working nor has nothing else to offer, people often turn to complementary therapies in desperation. Many therapies require a lot of training, but energy healing is one therapy that you can easily learn and do yourself. We are all hardwired for energy healing. Being able to offer your cherished pet healing not only helps the animal but helps you too. It transforms powerlessness and helplessness into hope. You now have a useful tool to help and that in itself is a relief when your pet is sick, injured or has been in an accident.

This book explains what energy healing is and how to do it.

Let's get started.

What is animal energy healing?

When an animal is ill, injured or traumatised (physically, mentally or emotionally) their life energy slows down or gets blocked. The purpose of energy healing is to re-establish the flow of energy and facilitate the animal healing themselves.

The healing we are studying could be called natural healing or energy healing. If your animal is sick, bring them to the conventional/holistic vet first. Energy healing is complementary to orthodox healing and is NOT a substitute for it. This means that if the animal has an infection, for example, they need to go to the vet and get antibiotics, or be treated by a homeopathic or holistic vet.

Once the animal has been seen by the vet, they can benefit from receiving energy healing. It can help boost their immune system so that *they heal themselves*.

How do I know if my animal is sick?

We have to observe the animal and learn first of all know what is normal for them. Then take prompt action if there is a change from the norm. Here is a list of common things to look out for. See Chapter 10 for information on a more comprehensive list.

- Is the animal urinating normally? Are they straining to urinate, trying to urinate frequently, or is there visible blood in their urine? Has a cat started urinating outside the litter box? Has a house trained pet started urinating indoors?

- Is their faeces normal, or are they constipated? Do they have diarrhoea, or is there blood in the faeces?

- Is their behaviour normal? Are they listless or not wanting to go for a walk? Have they stopped playing? Have they become aggressive when they are usually calm?

- Are they limping?

- Are they eating normally? Has their appetite diminished or disappeared? Are they making a sound of pain on eating?

- Is their weight stable or have they lost weight? Are they the right weight for their size?

- Are they coughing or vomiting?

- Are they drinking a lot more water than usual or not drinking at all?

- Are their eyes clear? Is there yellow or green pus coming from their eyes or nose?
- Is their coat shiny and groomed? Are they over grooming or pulling fur/hair out in clumps?
- Are they shaking their heads or scratching frequently?
- Are they indicating pain by whining or hiding under furniture?

Why learn how to do energy healing?

Being able to offer your animal energy healing is a wonderful way to help them recover faster. In addition to helping your animal heal itself, offering the healing helps you, the guardian, as it reduces the feeling of being powerless when your beloved pet is sick. So it is a win-win situation.

What does it take to learn energy healing?

It takes patience with yourself and your animal, love, compassion, a desire to help, and the willingness to practice. Many people who want to offer their own animals healing are sensitive. That can help in becoming proficient. What is also needed is the commitment to give yourself energy healing. The reason for this is to clear and recharge your energy body. You wouldn't expect to take a shower in

January and say, "I'm okay now till December!" No - you shower every day to keep your physical body clean. So the Self Care practice is about doing the same for your energy body.

Once you learn the basics from this book, the next step is to practice, practice and practice. The good news is that if you follow the guidelines set out, the healing that you are offering most definitely helps. It always helps in some way, but it is not always immediately obvious. It can help your pet feel better physically, emotionally, mentally and/or spiritually. I suggest that you allow yourself to trust that the energy healing is helping, as this is the most useful stance to take.

What may occur as a result of energy healing?

In my experience, healing takes place when there is a shift of stuck energy which is released from the animal. Sometimes the change is obvious and dramatic. The symptoms disappear and do not recur.

Often it is more subtle and becomes apparent over time in a process of gradual improvement. The animal may start eating again and put on weight. They may start playing again. They may show interest in life again, after they have lost a beloved companion animal - because of course, animals grieve the loss of their loved ones just like we do. Sometimes their behavioural problems lessen - but they benefit from dog training classes in addition to the healing.

When I work with a client I usually suggest a number of different strategies that experience has taught me will help. I have detailed these later in the book.

Sometimes healing means that the symptoms which have been causing pain, behavioural problems or physical illness resolve - but they come back when triggered by stress. Sometimes the animal dies - but with healing, they can die peacefully, surrounded by love. What more can any of us hope for when our time comes?

What I have found is that while there is no single magic bullet that will help "cure" all ills, energy healing *always helps on some level*. It's also important to understand that your animal is part of a unit. That unit consists of you, the guardian, the animal, and any other human/animal family members. So when I offer healing to an animal, I always ask the guardian can I direct energy to them as well - because you can rest assured whatever is going on with them affects their animal too.

The bottom line is that if you are stressed, they are stressed. If you are peaceful, it gives them the best energetic environment in which to recover. So please do not skip the self-care practices described. We are all connected by energy, so the clearer your energy, the higher your vibration, and the better it is for your beloved pet. By looking after your own energy and well-being, you are creating a field of healing energy around you. If you find it difficult to expend time and energy on yourself, you might consider reading and implementing the strategies outlined in my book, *How to Love Yourself in Less Than 50 Years.*

Does giving an animal healing guarantee that it will recover?

No, it does not. There are many factors that affect the recovery of a pet, including its age, previous illnesses or traumas, how long they have been sick, their diet, environment, normal level of vitality/immune system strength, and if it is their time to pass into spirit.

Can I give my pet healing instead of going to the vet?

No. I learned this from experience with my old cat Gannet. She had an eye infection which I just treated with energy healing. She went blind in that eye because I didn't bring her to the vet. Please learn from my mistakes. It's not either the vet or energy healing - there is a place for both. When your animal is sick, the first port of call is the vet, and then you can offer energy healing as supportive therapy. We have to be sensible and work on all levels for the best care of our animals. Work on the principle of "First, do no harm." Having said that, sometimes conventional vet treatment does not work, which is why I have listed complementary therapy options in Chapter 10. And to reiterate, energy healing always helps on some level.

Why bother to give animals that are terminally ill "healing"?

Because it can make their passing into spirit easier, more peaceful and gentle. And it can help you cope better with their transition too. There is such a thing as "dying a healed death."

Is it safe for me to do energy healing?

Yes - if you follow the guidelines in this book, especially those about Grounding and Self Care. If you have any fears about offering energy healing, then do not do it. Work on the principle "If in doubt, leave it out."

Are there any times or circumstances where it is not advisable?

Yes - if your animal has a broken bone, either send the energy to their Higher Self or wait until the bone is set. Otherwise, the healing can start before the bone has been reset in the correct position, and then the bone has to be broken again in order to be reset properly. Do not do hands-on healing on an area of broken skin or on a wound as it may hurt the animal. Hands-off or distant healing is just as effective as it works by intention. Also - do not do healing if you feel sick, exhausted, or have taken alcohol or recreational drugs.

How many healing sessions should I offer my pet?

As many as are needed until they are better. Then stop. You may find that when your animal needs a top up of healing energy, they will come to you for it. It is comforting for them as well as boosting their immune system. They absolutely LOVE having your full loving attention and that in itself is healing for your beloved pet.

A brief overview of energy healing

All living beings have the ability, design and tendency to heal themselves. They have self-balancing internal systems, e.g. the stress response amps up the system and the relaxation response calms it down. If you think about it, it is logical. How would species survive otherwise? However, various factors either contribute to this self-healing or get in the way of it. (See Chapter 9: Creating Conditions for Good Health.)

 In energy healing, there are only two possibilities:

- There is something harmful, detrimental or imbalanced in the energy field or body which needs to come out.
- There is something missing in the energy field or body which

needs to go in.

In this basic energy healing book, I show you how to safely direct healing energy into your pet. You could think of stuck energy like a pool of muddy water. A stream flowing into the pool for a period of time will disperse the mud and allow the water to become clear. That is the essence of basic energy healing - allowing the energy to flow through you so that it clears the energy system of your pet. Once you "pour" fresh energy in, you don't need to direct it. It knows where to go, because just as water always goes to the lowest level, the energy always flows to where the energy vibration is lowest.

When an animal is ill, shocked or traumatised, their energy signal is muted and at a low vibration. Think about it - they look sick, they are lifeless, not playing, not eating, and not moving. That is what a low energy vibration looks like.

Energy transfers from a higher vibration to a lower one, causing the lower one to rise. Then a process called entrainment causes the two different vibrations to match each other. You could think of a flat car battery being jump started from a full car battery. Both cars are up and running when the process is completed. When the two energies are matched it is called resonance. When the lower vibration rises, it lets the animal "kick start" their immune system and start to self-heal.

Another way to view energy is that when it is healthy it is coherent and organised. When it becomes stuck or sluggish, it becomes incoherent and discordant. Cancer is an extreme form of incoherent, discordant, disorganized energy. The purpose of healing is to help the animal get into their natural state of coherent energy.

Key Points

- All living beings have the ability, design and tendency to heal themselves.
- When your animal is sick, the first port of call is the vet, then offer energy healing as supportive therapy.
- The purpose of energy healing is to help the animal get into their natural state of coherent energy and facilitate them healing themselves.

Chapter 2

Energy Body 101

Every human, every animal, each blade of grass, each animate and even inanimate object has a luminous body that surrounds and interpenetrates it and emits its own characteristic radiation.
Joan Ranquet, Animal Healer

The universal energy field

The healing energy comes from the universal energy field (UEF) which surrounds all of us. Every human and every creature is composed of energy vibrating at a certain frequency. Even inanimate objects have an energy signature, because they too are composed of energy. The planet itself emits an energy signature. So we are surrounded by energy, made of energy and linked by a big web of energy. Fresh universal energy is naturally healing. You might also hear healing energy called qi, chi or prana. Different names, same thing. The energy is free, unlimited, and always available.

The aura or energy field

Each living thing has an energy field or aura around it and it interacts with the UEF. The aura is composed of layers which are often called "bodies." For example, the etheric body is a matrix of energy and is the layer closest to the physical body. It is connected to the physical body at the chakras. The next layer is called the astral body, or the emotional body. It contains the strong emotional memories of your pet, such as trauma or fear. There are other layers, but for the purpose of this book I will leave it at that.

The energy field is like a shield and a store. It acts in a similar way to the ozone layer that shields the earth from solar radiation. When it is intact and clear, the person/animal has a strong immune system and the ability to self-heal quickly. If it develops holes or tears in it, becomes brittle or has areas of stagnation, the immune system is weakened and the ability to self-heal is slowed down or absent.

The aura also acts as a store for the energy of trauma or abuse. When an animal suffers trauma of any sort, such as an accident, being abused, or being abandoned, they experience emotional shock in their nervous system. If it is processed and released, all is well once the physical body heals. Giving energy healing after a trauma can help prevent physical/behavioural symptoms from emerging, as well as assisting the animal to heal himself. It allows the trauma to be safely released.

If the shock or trauma is not discharged it then it stays in the energy field, and it works its way through the layers of the energy field into the physical body and creates physical, behavioural or psychological symptoms e.g. PTSD or anxiety post-trauma. There is a saying in therapy with humans: *The issues are in the tissues*. This means that anxiety, for instance, is located in the PHYSICAL body. It is in the cells.

Energy healing helps animals to release the shock from their cells, tissues, whole system and aura, and free up internal healing resources to help them get better. If there has been a big traumatic event, it is likely to require healing on an ongoing basis until the symptoms are relieved. Healing is usually a process, not a one-time event. Having said that, animals usually soak up the healing energy much faster than humans because they are open to it, and they have no hang-ups about it. They are not thinking, "This will never work." The majority of animals LOVE receiving energy healing because it feels safe, comforting and they know instinctively that it will help them. So a problem that might take ten one-hour sessions of energy healing to resolve in a human could take five twenty-minute sessions with an animal. All animals are unique individuals, however, so you need to just go with the flow.

Observe the outcome, and let yourself be guided by your animal too. Although the aura is invisible to the naked eye, it can be seen by people who are clairvoyant. It can also be seen by using Kirlian photography or gas discharge visualisation imaging.

Chakras

In humans and animals, the healing energy is taken into the body from the UEF via the chakras. The word chakra comes from the Sanskrit for "wheel."

Chakras are connectors to the subtle, invisible energy circulation system. They are the interface between the body and the universal energy field. They are spinning vortices of energy that pull universal energy into the body from the UEF.

There are seven main chakras or energy centres in the midline of the body from the top of the head to the tail bone. Each chakra is linked to an endocrine organ within the body, and to body structures close to those organs. Each chakra also corresponds to a colour, feelings, and behavior. It has an emotional issue linked to it, and is linked to a layer of the aura outside the physical body.

Within the body, the energy flows like a river. It is distributed through the body by energy channels called meridians. When it flows freely, the person/animal is healthy. When it is blocked, stagnant or stops flowing, symptoms occur.

The means by which energy healing is transmitted for energy healing is through the hands. Besides the seven main chakras, there are chakras in the palms of your hands. (Actually there are said to be 88,000 chakras in the body but let's keep it simple!)

Animals too have chakras in the centre of their paws. When they are ill, they often want to go out into the garden or park and lie on the grass. The reason for this is that they want to absorb the healing and grounding energy of the earth, which vibrates at 7.83 hertz through their paws, or through their direct contact with the earth. (We could learn a lot from our animal friends.)

Root or base chakra

Base of tail or spine; red; it relates to support, feeling safe in the world and survival issues. Most rescued animals need a lot of work on the root chakra to overcome the trauma they have experienced.

Sacral

Between lower abdomen and pelvis; orange; it relates to sexuality, reproduction, joy and the emotional body.

Solar plexus

Stomach; yellow; it relates to being able to take in and use energy, feeling powerful, and digestion issues.

Heart

Chest; green and pink; it relates to using energy from the lower and higher chakras, the chest and heart area, and love.

Throat

Turquoise; it relates to communication and expression.

Third eye or brow

Between the eyes; indigo; wisdom and intuition, also telepathic abilities. (Animals are naturally telepathic.)

Crown

Top of the head; violet; connection between the animal, its soul and the universal energies.

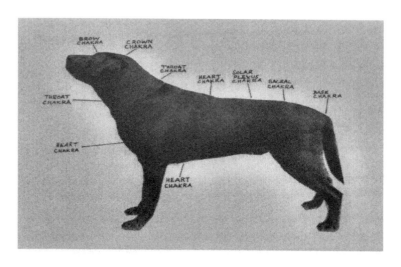

The nature of energy

Energy has a holographic and quantum nature. It is everywhere at the same time. It follows intention. Once you connect with the animal through your intention to offer him/her healing, the energy transfer is immediate. This means that hands-off and distant healing is possible because you do not have to be in physical contact with the animal for the transfer to occur.

Charlie's story

A woman called Olivia contacted me about her dog Charlie. He had been hit by a car. The vet had seen him and said that his leg might or might not heal. The leg was splinted and bandaged. Charlie was back home but had not eaten or drunk, and just sat staring out the window. I was out of the country at the time but I offered to do distant healing. I sat down and offered healing to Charlie. (You will learn how to do this in Chapter 4.) He accepted. I sent him healing for twenty minutes, which was all the time I could spare. Olivia texted me later that day to say that Charlie had started eating and drinking.

Key Points

- We are all part of a Universal Energy Field or UEF. That is where healing energy comes from.

- All living beings have an energy field or aura around them. When it is intact and clear, the person/animal has a strong immune system and the ability to self-heal quickly. If it develops holes or tears in it, becomes brittle or has areas of stagnation, the immune system is weakened and the ability to self-heal is slowed down or absent.

- In humans and animals, the healing energy is taken into the body from the UEF via spinning vortices called chakras. They are like connectors to the subtle, invisible energy circulation system which is within all living beings. The energy channels along which the energy flows are called meridians. The energy can slow down, become stuck or blocked.

- Energy healing is used to get the energy flowing

correctly again so that the animal can heal himself.

- Because of the quantum nature of energy, hands-off and distant healing is possible because you do not have to be in physical contact with the animal for the energy transfer to occur.

Chapter 3

Preparation is Key

God is in the details.

Ludwig Mies Van Der Rohe

If you want interior decoration done, any house painter will tell you that preparation is nine tenths of the work. Don't worry if you feel a bit daunted by seeing the amount of preparation needed before healing. It just looks long because it is written down! Once you get the hang of it, you can be ready to start healing in a couple of minutes. It becomes second nature with practice.

Is it always safe to offer my pet healing?

Yes, if they give their permission. I will explain how to ask in this chapter. The only time it is NOT advisable is if you are feeling sick, or have alcohol or recreational drugs taken. Also, do NOT work on an area with a broken bone unless it has already been set, or do hands-on healing on broken/inflamed skin. If in doubt, either (a) do hands-off healing and send it to the animal's higher self, who will know what to do with it or (b) use the principle, "If in doubt, leave it out," by which I mean do not offer the animal healing at that time.

Grounding: Be Here Now

It is absolutely imperative that you ground yourself before you start healing. Sometimes people have an image of a healer being a vague, airy-fairy person. They are talking about someone who is ungrounded. They are not in their body. I can assure you that if you do not want to be grounded, you should not do healing. To be grounded means that you are in your body and willing to pay attention to what is happening with your pet right here, right now. The most effective healers are those who are most grounded. This is because through intentional grounding or connecting with the earth, they are tapping in to the healing frequency of the earth which vibrates at 7.83 hertz. Experiments have shown that when offering healing, gifted healers unconsciously match the 7.83 hertz vibration. There are different ways to ground yourself. Here are two options:

Method 1

Imagine the roots of a wise old tree growing from your root chakra down through the legs, through the soles of your feet down deep into the earth, connecting you with the earth. Be present in the present moment for yourself and therefore for your animal.

Method 2

Imagine there is a grounding cord going from your root chakra down into the centre of the earth. Expand this cord to the width of your body. Imagine it connects with blue healing light at the centre of the earth and that healing energy comes back up from it, filling your feet, legs, knees and root chakra the base of the spine, between the legs. Imagine this is a continuous circuit of supportive, healing energy for you. Set it on a timer to Automatic, Constant, and 100%.

Tap in to universal energy

This is where you make sure you are using Universal Energy (the equivalent of WI-FI or unlimited broadband) versus your Personal Energy, (the equivalent of Data on your phone) which is limited and would leave you depleted. Take three deep calming breaths to centre your energy. Imagine the Cosmic/Christ/God/Universal energy coming down through the top of your head, down to your neck, down your arms, and out your hands. This is the energy you will be using for healing. If you want to think of the source of energy healing in a different way, imagine a grid of healing energy around the planet. According to healer Jeffrey Allen, this is the source of energy for healing work. However you choose to tap into the source of it, imagine it coming down through the top of your head, down to your neck, down your arms, and out your hands. There are chakras or energy vortices in the palms of your hands. You will use your hands to direct the energy.

Intention

It is really, really, really important that you set a clear intention for your healing, because energy follows intention. Set your intention that the healing will now begin to flow, and that it is for "the highest good of all concerned and in divine order." That way, you can't go wrong. I suggest that you learn this phrase by heart, and use it always.

Protection for your energy field

We are constantly bombarded with signals and information. These can be vocal, emotional or behavioural from the people around us. They can be the ads on the TV, radio and internet that are designed to persuade us to buy something, do something or be something other than who we are. The litany of bad news on the nightly news has a negative effect on our life energy. The media content that we consume, the video games we play, the books we read - they all either boost or deplete our energy to get through the day. It is estimated that we receive more information in one week than our prehistoric ancestors did in their whole lives. It can be overwhelming, because although our technology has sped up, our limbic (reptilian) brain is the same as millennia ago. We are in constant fight or flight mode due to perceived threats. So use your discernment if you feel exhausted, and ask, "Is this helping me or draining me?"

A few years ago, I found myself getting depressed by the news on the TV. So I decided to do a "news fast" for a month. I noticed an increase in my life energy. That was seven years ago, and I never restarted listening to the news! I can guarantee you, if it is bad enough, someone will tell you about it, or you will see snippets as you surf the web.

So it is a good idea to protect your energy field from external negativity. Generally speaking, once you protect your energy field it remains protected for 24 hours. If you know that you are going into a difficult situation you can do a top up to give you confidence if you wish.

Protecting your energy field is easy to do and there are many ways to do it. The important thing is to choose one and use it. Here are three ways to do it:

Method 1

Visualise a protective blue or white light completely surrounding your energy field, in all directions, including above your head and below your feet, like a cloak or giant egg.

Method 2

Use a prayer such as: I call on Archangel Michael to protect my energy field today. Thank you.

Method 3

The governing meridian is the name given to an energy channel in your body. It runs from the middle of the upper lip over the head and down to the base of the spine. Use a magnet (such as a fridge magnet) and roll it from between your eyes, over the head to the shoulders, while holding the intention of putting a shield up.

Tune in to your heart

The heart has an electromagnetic field that is 5000 times more powerful than the brain. So tapping into this field of energy increases the power of the healing. Focus your attention on your heart chakra by placing your right hand on your heart. Bring to mind an animal or person you love unconditionally. Feel gratitude towards that being. Let the feelings of love and gratitude expand until they fill your whole body and aura. Doing this raises your vibration and allows the healing energy to flow more easily through you.

Permission

Here are two ways to ask permission from the animal to offer healing:

Method 1

Mentally ask permission of the animal to send them healing. Trust what the response is, and only offer healing if the animal agrees.

Method 2

Start the healing and if your animal looks or acts agitated or leaves the room, stop, and do hands-off healing to your pet's higher self, who will direct the energy wisely and well.

One of my cats, Harry Three Paws, only climbs up on my lap when he wants healing. The rest of the time he is like a teenager: "Uuh, I'm off. Here's my laundry!" When he does climb on my lap, I don't need to ask him permission because I know the drill. You and your animal may come up with a similar shortcut.

Self-healing first

If you are on an airplane with a child and the oxygen masks drop, you are always instructed to put your own oxygen mask on first, before you attend to your child. Otherwise you could pass out from lack of oxygen and you would be of no use to anyone. It is the same with healing. Charge up your own energy field first. Then start healing. This practice raises your vibration and makes you a more effective healer.

Close your eyes and take three calming deep breaths to centre yourself. Imagine that Cosmic or Christ energy (or God energy, Earth Healing Grid energy or whatever you wish to call it) is coming down from the Universe and in through the crown of your head. It comes to your neck and branches out down the arms and out through your hands. Hold your hands on your lap, facing each other. Let the cosmic energy flow into them and create a ball of white light between your hands. Let it build up for about five minutes. Direct this energy into yourself for at least five minutes.

Offering Healing

See Chapter 4 for step-by-step instructions.

Closing down

A friend told me about doing healing on her cat that had joint pain. The cat appeared much more comfortable after the healing but the friend now had pain in her wrist. This is because she didn't know how to ground and close down safely.

Close the animal's chakras

Visualise the animal's chakras closing down, one by one, with a cross of white light on each one, and that they are surrounded by a blue cloak of protective energy.

Disconnect your energy

When you finish your healing, imagine you are drawing your energy back in around you. Ground yourself again. Imagine you are detaching or breaking the healing link between you and the animal. Use a ritual like washing your hands to signify to the universe that you are finished for now and that you are "turning off the energy tap."

Close your chakras

Imagine your chakras are closed down and sealed with a cross, and that you are surrounded by a blue cloak of protective energy.

Ground yourself again.

- E.g. Imagine the roots of a wise old tree growing from your root chakra down through the legs, through the soles of your feet down deep into the earth, connecting you with the earth.

- Drinking a glass of water also helps you to be grounded.

Clear your energy field

Clear off your energy field by brushing it off and shaking off your hands. Ask the Archangel Michael to clear your energy field too. Drink plenty of water e.g. 6-8 glasses in 24 hours after you do a healing session to flush your system out.

Checklist before Healing:

- Are you Grounded and fully present?
- Have you tapped into Universal Energy?
- Have you set a clear intention for the healing?
- Have you tuned in to your heart?
- Is your aura protection in place?
- Have you asked permission of the animal?
- Have you done at least five minutes of self-healing?

Checklist after Healing:

- Have you disconnected your energy from the animal?
- Have you closed the animal's chakras?
- Have you closed your own chakras?
- Have you grounded yourself again?
- Have you cleared your energy field?

Key Points

- There are vital procedures to do before you start healing, in order to do it safely.

- Get into the habit of going through the checklist before you start and when you finish.

- The preparation is the groundwork to become a competent and safe energy healer for animals.

Chapter 4

Offering Healing

*The ability of humans to tap into and deliver unseen energies
is the fundamental basis of all energy healing.*
Harry Edwards, famous English spiritual healer

How to offer healing

Once you have gone through your preparation checklist,
turn the phone off so that you can focus your attention on
your pet. Make yourself comfortable so that you can hold
your position for a while and set aside about 20 minutes. It
could take more or less time. Every animal is different.

Case history of Noelle with amputated leg

Noelle was a kitten of about six months when she came into
the sanctuary. She had a front leg and part of her tail
amputated probably due to a car accident. She just lay in the
cage, not moving and eating very little. That is what an
animal in shock looks like - frozen. I took her home for some
TLC. She was very scared at first and didn't want me

touching her so I did hands-off healing. After a week of this she started to engage with me and started to play. I changed then to hands-on healing. One of the things I did was to direct healing to where the leg would have been if it had not been amputated, and the same with the tail. The purpose of this was to relieve and release any phantom pain. Kirlian photography shows that if a leaf is cut off a plant, the energetic imprint remains for some time. It is the same with animals and humans, and that is why phantom pain can be experienced. She really loosened up then and started running around the house playing.

Breathe

Breathing deeply and evenly, let the breath be as it is. No need to force it, just make sure that you are breathing deeply. This triggers the relaxation response. You will know when this has been triggered as you will become aware of extra saliva in your mouth. When you are relaxed, the healing energy flows more easily through you. When you are tense, you breathe through the top one third of your lungs and your body tension blocks the energy. Deep abdominal breathing triggers the relaxation response. You are aiming to ALLOW the healing flow easily and effortlessly through you. You are not trying to force anything as this is counterproductive.

Relax while healing

The energy is intelligent. It goes to where it is needed most. Just relax and focus on sending love to your animal. Be present in the present moment with your pet. The essence of energy healing is being calm, still, grounded, quiet and radiating love with the intention to help your pet heal himself. If it can be unconditional love like your pet offers you, even better. Just do your best. It doesn't have to be perfect. Relax and trust that it will help, because it always does help at some level - physical, mental, emotional or spiritual. Your animal will be delighted with your undivided attention and it will strengthen the love bond between you. Now you are (finally!) ready to start the healing!

Comfort and safety of your pet

Make sure the animal is safe and cannot roll onto the floor or hurt themselves. If your pet is small, put a cushion on your lap and see if your pet will sit there. If not, work on your pet where they are. Get down on the floor if necessary, and make yourself as comfortable as possible, because once you start it is best to continue without interrupting.

How to offer hands-on healing

There are a number of ways to do it, all equally valid. Try what works best for you. Relax! Smile! The more relaxed your body is, the easier it is for the energy to flow through you. If you are tense, worried, and thinking, "Am I doing this right? What if I get it wrong?" you are creating resistance to the flow of the energy. Once you have followed the guidelines, you are DEFINITELY doing it right. Energy follows intention. Don't overthink it. Just do it. Enjoy!

Tip on hand positioning

If possible, make an "energy sandwich" with your hands, palms facing each other, with the animal's body in between your hands. This increases the power of the healing. If it is not possible, don't worry about it. Your best is good enough.

How to offer hands-on healing - Method 1

Start by placing your hands on the crown chakra between the ears. If the animal is small, your hand may well cover both the crown and brow chakra. That's fine. The energy goes to where it is needed. Stay in each area for three to five minutes. If you feel you should stay in a certain area longer, do that.

Move to the throat. Put your hands each side of the throat if you can.

Move to the heart, and if you can, put your hands on the front of the chest as well as at the back, making an "energy sandwich."

For the solar plexus, put one hand on the back of the body at the centre of the spine. This covers the adrenal glands that secrete the stress hormone and in rescue animals often needs a lot of work. If possible, place the other hand at the front of the body in the "energy sandwich" position. If it is not possible, hold the other hand off to the side, palm facing the first hand.

Move to the root chakra, placing one hand on the base of the tail.

The animal may move around to indicate where it wants healing, and if it does this, follow its lead. Dogs especially often reverse in to your hands as if to say, "Here's my bottom. Start here!" When they do this they want you to start work on their root chakra. They instinctively prioritise where they want to feel the energy. Just relax and go with the flow.

The healing is usually finished when the animal moves away, but sometimes they take a short break and come back for more. Wait and see what happens.

How to offer hands-on healing - Method 2

Just put your hands on your animal in a comfortable way. Let the healing flow. When they have had enough, they will move away from you. Sometimes pets, especially dogs, move away for a small break. After a few minutes they may come back for more.

How to offer hands-off healing

There are many times when it is preferable to use hands-off healing. These include the preference of your animal, safety issues e.g. with a traumatised animal, or if there is an animal in a cage or tank. It is also useful for wild animals. Always be mindful of your own safety.

Method

Having gone through the checklist, if you have an animal in a cage or tank, just place your hands on the outside of the cage or tank. If your pet wants healing but doesn't want to be touched, just leave them where they are and send them healing from where you are sitting. It makes no difference whether you are touching them or not. The healing works through your intention.

Note to animal sanctuary healers

In an ideal world, when you go to offer healing to animals in a sanctuary, you would have a quiet space to work in, no interruptions and plenty of time.

In the real world that has not been my experience. So I suggest that you do your healing preparation before you leave home and then you are ready to work on arrival. When you finish with one animal, flick off your hands and fingers to break the energy between you and the animal, before you start work on the next one. When I do healing in the Dog's Aid sanctuary, I always set my intention that as the healing goes into one animal, it goes out to them all, and they are free to tune into it and absorb it if they wish. I do it this way because I never have enough time to offer individual healing to all the animals that need it, and it is the best I can do.

If you run short of time, sit down and send distant healing to all the animals in the sanctuary using the intention of "that they may all be healed in accordance with their highest good and in divine order."

How to send distant healing

Distant healing - Method 1

Having gone through the checklist, and received permission from the animal, bring the animal to mind and let the healing flow. It makes no difference whether you are touching them or not. The healing works through your intention. Some people find it easier to focus on a photo of the animal as they work. Place your hands on your lap facing each other and imagine a miniature version of the animal is in between them. If you have time, send healing to one animal at a time. If you are pressed for time, imagine all the recipients in between your hands at the same time. Send the healing for a time period such as 15 minutes, 20 minutes, half an hour or an hour. Usually an hour is the maximum an animal will take or need, but every case is different.

Case history of Sam the cat with bladder crystals

Crystals can build up in the bladder, usually in a male cat, and break down into a fine sandy substance which blocks the urethra. It may be called bladder crystals or FUS, Feline Urologic Syndrome. It can be life threatening and quite often conventional vet medicine has little to offer. A friend had to have her cat put to sleep after repeated blockages. I came across this healing meditation and it has worked to help a number of cats with blockages. After you have taken your cat to the vet for treatment, you can do this healing yourself to try to help things along for your pet.

A friend contacted me about her cat Sam who had been diagnosed with bladder crystals. The vet said it was not looking good. I was many miles from Sam but I did distant healing on him as follows: Having gone through the checklist and received permission from Sam, I imagined he was sitting on my knee. I placed my hands in an energy-sandwich position around his imaginary lower body. I imagined the healing energy flowing through my hands and into his kidneys and down into his bladder. I imagined the sandy substance being made into even smaller, finer sand that could be washed out through the urethra. I did this for 20 minutes, three times a day. The next day he passed urine and the condition has not recurred at the time of writing.

Healing for bladder crystals in cats

Switch off the phone and go through your checklist. Visualise the cosmic energy coming down through the crown chakra to your throat, down your arms into your hands and out through them. Build up the ball of energy between your hands. If you are with your cat in person, and he will allow you, place your hands on his bladder, forming an "energy sandwich" with the bladder in between the hands. So the hands can be on either side of the body, for instance. Then send the energy into the bladder and visualise it breaking up the crystals. Imagine the crystals being blown up or dissolved and then flowing easily and effortlessly out the urethra as the cat does a pee.

Be sure to focus on what you do want - the cat doing a pee - as opposed to the pictures of what has NOT been happening - the cat straining to use the litter tray. If your mind wanders, don't worry. Just go back to focusing on the healing as soon as you realise it has wandered and let go of any need to give out to yourself for the natural tendency of the mind to wander. Use a pale blue colour to reduce any pain or inflammation. Keep this up for as long as your cat stays on your knee. When you are finished, ground and close down as usual.

Distant healing - Method 2

If there is someone with the animal while you are away, ask the person to act as a proxy. Ask them to sit down with the animal either on their lap or close by. If the animal will allow, ask the proxy to put their hands gently on the affected area. Then you send the healing to the animal via the proxy. The advantage of this method is that you can get feedback from the person on the scene.

How to send distant healing in a group

Doing energy healing on your own is powerful and effective. Joining with others to offer healing hands-on, hands-off or through distant healing is exponentially more powerful. You can join with a group of like-minded individuals to practice the methods outlined and then agree a focus for the healing. For example, I trained a number of people from the animal sanctuary I volunteer in, Dog's Aid, to do basic energy healing. The training I gave them is similar to the contents of this book. When I need help for an animal, I ask the team to send distant healing to that animal. We have a WhatsApp group and I send them a photo of the animal with a short outline of the situation. If you are going to work with a team like this, it is also important to give updates on the recipient so that people can see how they are helping and remain motivated.

Case history of group distant healing

A German Shepherd dog called Bella came into the sanctuary. She had picked up a firework in her mouth and it had exploded. She was brought to the vet immediately. He didn't hold out much hope for her and said she might have to be put to sleep. He treated her with an antibiotic injection and asked for her to be brought back in two days. I happened to be in the sanctuary when she was brought in. She was very shocked and traumatised. I worked on her with hands-on energy healing and also used the Emotion Code (see the Emotion Code information in Chapter 10.) I used the advanced technique of drawing off (see Energy Scan and Drawing Off in Chapter 6.) I took a photo of her and asked the Distant Healing team to send her healing. I gave her a homeopathic remedy of Aconite for shock and pain, and Arnica for bruising and shock.

She was brought back to the vet as requested and given another antibiotic injection. At this stage she was drinking water but not eating. Maggie who runs the sanctuary tried her with various mushy wet foods and she started eating a little. I did another hands-on session with her the following week. She went on to make a complete recovery with no apparent traumatic residue. This was due to the combination of good vet care, antibiotics, homeopathy, hand-feeding, TLC, close monitoring - and the group energy healing which cleared her energy field of the shock and trauma and freed up her internal resources to let her fully recover.

Closing down

When finished, do the Closing Down ritual as detailed below. The procedure is the same for hands-on, hands-off or distant healing.

Close the animal's chakras

Visualise the animal's chakras closing down, one by one, with a cross of white light on each one.

Disconnect your energy

When you finish your healing, imagine you are drawing your energy back in around you. Ground yourself again. Imagine you are detaching or breaking the healing link between you and the animal. Use a ritual like washing your hands to signify to the universe that you are finished for now and that you are "turning off the energy tap."

Close your chakras

Imagine your chakras are closed down and sealed with a cross, and that you are surrounded by a blue cloak of protective energy.

Ground yourself again

- E.g. Imagine the roots of a wise old tree growing from your root chakra down through the legs, through the soles of your feet down deep into the earth, connecting you with the earth.

- Drinking a glass of water also helps you to be grounded.

Clear your energy field

Clear off your energy field by brushing it off and shaking off your hands. Ask the Archangel Michael to clear your energy field too. Drink plenty of water e.g. 6-8 glasses in 24 hours after you do a healing session to flush your system out.

Case history of Harry Three Paws

One of my cats is Harry Three Paws. He is very famous as he even has his own book, *The Tale of Harry Three Paws!* He is

now eight years old and he had his right hind leg amputated as a kitten after a car accident. That happened before I met him in the animal sanctuary I volunteer in as a healer. He is an amazing character and prefers interacting with people as opposed to cats. Because of the missing leg, his spine is constantly out of balance.

He is extremely independent but when he comes to sit on my knee, I know that he wants healing. He could take up to an hour and a half of healing at a time. Then he might not want any for three weeks.

When he lies on the sofa in the wintertime, I often use a flexible microwaveable heat pack for him. I heat it up for one minute, sprinkle two drops of lavender oil on it for relaxation, and place it along the length of his spine. This helps ease the muscles and keeps him mobile so that he can visit his human friends the next day. I also give him one capsule of cod liver oil every second day.

Key Points

- Make sure that you and your pet are comfortable before you start to offer healing.

- Make sure that you are safe, if working with wild animals or animals that you do not know.

- The more relaxed you are, the easier it is for the healing to flow through you.

- You can choose to offer hands-on, hands-off or distant healing to your pet or any animal, once you have followed the guidelines. All are effective.

- When you are finished, close down and ground.

Chapter 5

You & Your Pet During Healing

The most beautiful thing we can experience is the mysterious.
Albert Einstein

What to expect

When you have the experience of offering an animal healing and can see the difference it makes to them, your heart will be full. But it is important to remember that you may not actually see any visible difference immediately. This chapter describes the variations of experience that you and your pet may encounter during the healing process.

Case history of Timmy

A five month old puppy called Timmy was hit by a car. He had a punctured lung, a broken pelvis, and a broken leg. When he was released from the vet hospital his guardian asked me to do a healing session on him. He soaked up an hour of healing and my hands got so hot I was sure that if I plunged them into ice water steam would hiss out! He went

51

on to make a full recovery. If your hands get over-hot while healing, I have since learned that it is useful to "flick off" the energy from the hands.

What you may experience while healing

- You may feel heat or tingling in your hands while working.

- One hand may be hot while the other is cold.

- You may yawn, sigh, burp or pass wind while healing. If this happens it is the stuck energy in your pet's energy field being released through your own energy field. Your body makes you yawn/sigh/burp to release it and take in more oxygen. Many years ago I attended a training workshop in Integrated Energy Healing. The teacher burped so loudly as she was doing the initiation I found it hard to stop giggling! It was a Homer Simpson type burp, not a small delicate one. That's energy for you!

- You may feel tired during the healing, especially if there is significant energy being cleared. When this happens to me, I have noticed that once I complete the healing and close down correctly, my energy level stabilises and I feel fine again. If this happens to you while you are still learning, just take extra water and extra rest after you finish and close down.

- You may feel tingles or sensations of energy around your

body.

- You may get the feeling that you are being helped, especially if you have called in your guides or angels.

- You may get the feeling that you should keep your hands in one spot for a while. Follow your intuition.

How your pet may look or act during healing

- Your pet may yawn, sigh or fall asleep while you are working. The healing will work whether they are asleep or awake.

- Your pet may move away from you for a break and then come back for more.

- As mentioned, dogs may manoeuvre themselves so that their bottom is between your hands, or move your hands around so that they direct where your hands are. That is fine.

After healing

There are various reactions that you may observe in your pet following healing. Here are things to look out for, and be aware that they are part of the normal reaction to healing and are not of concern.

- Your pet may drink a lot of extra water and pee a lot for about 24 hours.

- Your pet may start eating immediately after the healing. This can be very helpful if you have an animal with kidney failure, for instance, where appetite loss is chronic.

- Healing Crisis: Be aware that your animal may become very lethargic after healing, or their condition may worsen temporarily, e.g. for 24 hours. This is a normal part of the healing process and is called an aggravation. It used to be common knowledge for instance, that a high temperature needed to peak before it broke, but many people have forgotten that now.

- There may be no apparent reaction at all. However, you can rest assured that the animal has been helped in some way - it just may be subtle, or take a couple of days to show improvement.

- Your pet may be wired to the moon and very hyperactive.

- Your pet may be very tired and sleep for a few hours

depending on the amount of trauma released. Sometimes they can sleep most of the time for the following two days, just getting up to drink, eat a little or pee.

- Your pet may be less interested in food for a day or two. Digestion takes a lot of energy and an animal may instinctively rest the gut while the healing is absorbed into the body.

Case history of Freckles the sheep

Recently I was doing healing on a sheep called Freckles at the local city farm. She was born with two deformed front legs. She was eating grain when I started doing the healing. After a while she relaxed so much that she just keeled over on her side and fell asleep. She woke up when I finished and started eating again. The feedback was that she was in great form afterwards.

Key Points

- You may feel heat, cold or tingling in your hands as you do the healing.

- Your pet may fall asleep during the healing, and this is fine.

- The symptoms may worsen temporarily before clearing.

- Your pet may have no apparent reaction to the healing, may be extra tired or hyperactive.

Chapter 6

Advanced Techniques

There are more things in heaven and earth, Horatio,
than are dreamt of in your philosophy.

William Shakespeare

Four optional extras

The energy healing already described is powerful and effective on its own, but here are some optional extras you might choose to add in. I suggest that you try out each one and see what appeals to you. If you feel it helps, include it in your normal healing practice. If not, let it go.

Energy scan and drawing off

If you have an animal with for instance, inflammation or an injury, after you have prepared in the usual way, run your hands about 10-15 centimetres above their body to do an Energy Scan. You may feel, or get a sense of an area of cold, heat or tingling. This indicates an area where the life force is stuck, blocked or sluggish. Use your left hand to work above the blockage, about 10-15 centimetres again, making anticlockwise circles and then wiping the energy off your left hand with your right hand. Imagine the discarded energy going into the Violet Flame for transformation and release, or going into the Earth where it is safely recycled. (The Violet Flame is associated with St. Germain and is a useful tool for safely releasing stuck energy.) Boyle's Law states that energy cannot be created or destroyed, it just changes form. Do this "drawing off" for a couple of minutes, then proceed as normal to replace the removed energy with fresh healing energy.

Every night, one of my cats, Felicity, has her Crazy Hour. One night she got behind the curtain and was attacking Harry Three Paws who couldn't get away from her. I put my hands down to try and relocate her so that poor Harry could escape and she scratched me badly on the wrist. After I stopped the bleeding, I drew off the energy and released it from my energy field, and did some healing on it. An hour later it wasn't even sore.

Colour healing

If you wish, as you are offering your pet healing, you can imagine colours flowing from your hands into your pet. If you are going to do this, please make sure that you use the PALEST TINT POSSIBLE of healing energy. If there is inflammation, imagine a pale blue going in and cooling everything down. If there is a lack of energy, imagine pale orange lifting the energy.

You can choose to imagine the appropriate colour for each chakra. Do not use red for the root, it is too strong - use a baby pink instead. Your animal is very sensitive to energy and will take what he/she needs. Pale orange for the sacral, yellow for the solar plexus, pale pink and green for the heart, turquoise for the throat, indigo for the third eye or forehead, violet for the crown.

Connecting with your healing team

When tapping in to energy healing, feel free to ask your angels to help. All living beings have an angel to mind them. There are 144,000 unnamed angels who are powerful and are just waiting to be asked to help. Ask them for help politely - and out loud.

You also have a spirit guide, or indeed a number of them, whether you are aware of them or not. Ask them for help too.

When you finish the healing session and have closed down, remember to thank your angels and spirit helpers for their assistance.

I work as a healer/therapist for humans as well as animals. On many occasions, a client has said to me after the session, "That was lovely.....but I don't understand - you were working on my feet and I could feel you at my head at the same time." I explain that while I was doing the feet, one of my healing guides was working on their head. (I haven't mastered the art of bilocation - yet!) My viewpoint is that when help is available, I will gladly ask for it for the benefit of my human and animal clients.

Crystal healing

Crystal healing is the subject of many entire books. The concept behind it is that crystals act as electromagnetic amplifiers of energy. If you are going to use crystals, watch your animal carefully. If they move away from the crystals or seem upset by them, don't use this method.

A simple approach is to use four crystals. You might choose either clear quartz crystal or rose quartz which has a gentle energy. Remember your animal is very sensitive to energies. Clear your crystals by rinsing them under running water or blessing them with a prayer. You can also imagine them being immersed in white light, or sound a tuning fork to clear them. Any method is fine. If you are using different crystals, make sure they are not water soluble if you are going to rinse them in water.

Program your crystals by holding them in your hands and stating your intention, e.g. "I now program you to help me heal this animal in accordance with his highest good and in divine order."

Set up your crystal grid with four clear quartz crystals with the pointed end directed in towards the animal. This energises their aura. Put one near the pet's head, one near the base of the tail, one to the left and one to the right, a few centimetres away from the body.

Prepare for your energy healing as usual and do the healing. When you are finished, close down as usual. Take the crystals and clean them again. Place them on a window ledge in the moonlight to recharge for 24 hours every 2 weeks if you are using them regularly.

Key Points

Here are four additional resources you might choose to add in to your healing work.

- Energy scan and drawing off
- Colour healing
- Connecting with your healing team
- Crystal healing

Chapter 7

Terminally Ill Pets

*Love is the most powerful
and still the most unknown energy of the world.*
Pierre Teilhard de Chardin

How to cope

Our pets have a shorter lifespan than us, so it is inevitable that we will be bereaved at some time. There is little acceptance of death in western culture, and much fear around a terminal diagnosis and the prospect of death.

It is likely, as pet guardians, that at some point we will have to make the decision to have our pet put to sleep or euthanized by the vet. This is a horrendously complex emotional dilemma: we don't want to see them suffer, but yet we love them so much. We feel their immense unconditional love for us. We don't want to lose that love either. But how do you kill the one you love and survive emotionally afterwards?

The answer is that there is no simple answer. I have

accompanied many animals on their last journey to the vet and it never gets easier. I do know this though: if I can stay grounded and present for them, and offer them healing throughout the process, it brings calmness to them. I have felt the quality of the atmosphere change and become more tranquil in the vet's room. Others have commented on the change too.

If your pet is given a terminal diagnosis, ask the vet how long have they got and if they are in pain just now? Because bringing them home, if you have a chance to do so, can give you time to say goodbye to your friend.

It might be advisable to ask the vet to come to your home to have your pet put to sleep. It can be emotionally overwhelming to have it done in the vet's surgery. In my local vet's, they light a candle and have a sign up requesting quiet out of respect for an animal that is being euthanized. Or the vet tries to schedule the appointment to avoid the crowds. These things are worth considering - be as kind to your heart as possible.

The purpose of Rescue Remedy flower essence is to calm, comfort and reassure. I put a drop on the back of the neck of the animal (it can be absorbed through the energy field) and take some myself (sub lingually, i.e. under the tongue) to steel myself to get through the process.

It is worth considering what your beliefs are about what happens after we die. After a lifetime of metaphysical study, my belief is that consciousness survives death, for both humans and animals. The human or animal body is left behind at death and the person or animal goes into spirit. Our pets are often looked after by our loved human family that has passed over already. Or they are lovingly minded by "animal people" or helpers in spirit. We will be reunited with our pets and human loved ones when we too pass into spirit.

Millie's story

Millie is a 15 year old mixed breed dog, a lovely old girl with a gentle nature. A lump on her back leg was cancerous and the vet felt she only had a few weeks left. Her guardian Mary asked me to come and do some healing on Millie, which I did. Weeks turned to months and we established a routine of a healing session every few weeks. Mary made changes to her lifestyle which included working from home. Millie was very happy with this change and very contented in her special bed in the home office. She continued on the tablets from the vet. 15 months later, she was able for a 7 hour car journey (done with plenty of breaks) to a holiday down the country. Her eyes were clear, her coat glossy, her appetite was good and she was in no pain or distress. The lump on her leg was now the size of a small melon but it appeared to be stable. She has now outlived the terminal diagnosis by two years and is still alive at the time of writing with a good quality of life.

Millie's story shows that sometimes our animal friends can live well even with a terminal diagnosis. Making the most of the time left and evaluating the situation on an on-going basis seems to be the key in cases like this.

Staying calm and grounded

When our pet is hurt in an accident, it helps them for us to stay grounded and as calm as possible. For us to lose the plot and become very emotional is just not helpful. We will have time after the crisis to process the event and release our feelings (and we should do this for our own self-care) by crying, talking to a friend or writing it down.

Cassie and Dodie's story

On one occasion I went to Dog's Aid animal sanctuary and Maggie, who runs it, asked me to tune in to an elderly dog called Cassie and see if she was ready to go into spirit, and if she wanted to be helped by a vet. Cassie was in her bed and her friend Dodie was in the bed beside her. I did as I had been asked and the first thing that came back was an overwhelming wave of gratitude and love for Maggie. It brought tears to my eyes. The second thing that came back was that she wasn't quite ready to go, but not long now. I said out loud to Cassie that was fine, and if she wanted to go in her sleep that was okay too. Sometimes our animals need to know that we can let them go, that they are free to go and that they don't have to worry about us. I offered her some healing and she accepted it. I also sent healing ahead to the time of her passing, asking that it be gentle, swift and merciful and that she would be helped by angels. When I do healing in the sanctuary, I always set my intention that as the healing goes into one animal, it goes out to them all, and they are free to tune into it and absorb it if they wish. The following week I was back again and I asked Maggie how Cassie was. "She's fine," she said, but the morning after you left I found Dodie dead in her bed." So Dodie had tuned into the conversation and taken it on board too.

Finding the right time to let go

Because we are so emotionally connected to our beloved pet, it can be difficult for us to know when the right time is to have a pet put to sleep. In truth, all we can do is hold in mind the intention of doing the best we can for our beloved animal.

In the wild, cats are prey for larger carnivores so they instinctively hide their pain or sickness as a survival strategy. Sick or injured animals get killed quicker than healthy ones. It can really help to have a trusted friend or vet who can assess the situation on an on-going basis. The questions are: Is the animal in pain? Is he suffering? How does he look? What is his quality of life now?

How to know if your pet is in pain

Cats

- Running away from the guardian

- Hiding under furniture

- Loss of appetite

- Appearing quieter than usual, depressed, cold, pinched, lethargic, as if they have given up

- Just not themselves or less social

- Change in behaviour

- Not playing anymore

- Moving around less

- Litter box accidents

- Fur looking dull, matted or clumped or standing up on a cat's back so that it looks separated

- Whimpering/jumping when starting to eat, indicating possible mouth or dental problem

Dogs

- Some dogs show their pain and some dogs hide it. Signs to look out for to check if your dog is in pain include:

- Depression, lethargy, lack of movement

- Change in behaviour

- Limping or whimpering

- Loss of appetite

- Panting without having exercised

- Not wanting to socialise or go for a walk

- Some dogs become more needy when in pain and want more attention

Gannet's story

Gannet was my old cat mentioned in the Introduction. To recap, she was diagnosed with squamous cell carcinoma on her ear. I got one ear removed and then the cancer appeared on the second ear. I brought her to a healer to see if that

could help and although she was feral, she totally relaxed
when getting the healing, which was very unusual. I tried to
catch her to bring her back for more work but I couldn't, and
that was how and why I learned about energy healing. Once
I started to offer her healing, we got into a routine. She
would sit on my lower legs and accept the healing for as
long as she wanted. She was a feral cat, and although she
had known me for sixteen years at this stage, she wouldn't
want to take the chance of actually sitting on my knee. No
way!

The cancer on her ear seemed to subside and did not spread.
I asked Emily McAteer, a homeopathic vet, to come to visit
her and see was there anything she could do to improve the
quality of her life. Emily gave me some remedies for Gannet

which seemed to perk her up and make her more comfortable. Then she developed chronic kidney failure. As my local vet, Denis says, "If they live long enough, all cats get some degree of kidney failure." She was on Fortecor tablets daily, and a special low-protein, low-phosphorus food. Her appetite was poor and she had to be coaxed to eat. That is not unusual with a cat in renal failure. I noticed that immediately after her healing, she often ate some food. Then she started going downhill and needed subcutaneous fluids every second day. Because I was a qualified nurse, the vet allowed me to give her the fluids at home. I continued to give her energy healing every day, sometimes for hours. This went on for 17 months and she was stable.

The week before Christmas Gannet gave me a clear signal that we had come to the end of the road. When I went to give her the subcutaneous fluids, she miaowed and hissed angrily. She had never done that before. Clearly she had had enough. With a heavy heart, I rang Denis the vet. "Once you take her off the medications and the drip, Marese, she'll be gone in ten days. Ring me if you need me to put her to sleep." I put the phone down and burst into tears. My long-time furry friend was going to die. I knew it was coming but still, you are never ready.

I pulled myself together and said, "Right. If you are going to die, Gannet, let's forget this renal food that you don't like." I cancelled Christmas and went shopping for food. Free range chicken, turkey, wild salmon - you name it, if I thought she would eat it, I bought it. Nothing to lose now. I prepare it

71

lovingly and offer her morsels. To my surprise, she begins to nibble at it, and drink the free range chicken broth I had made. I was surprised but pleased. I wanted her last few days to be as comfortable as possible. That evening we sat as usual, with her on my lap as I listened to soothing light classical music. I gave her energy healing as I had many times before. We sat together for ages, and I only got up when I needed food or the bathroom. That was Day One, and the clock was ticking.

Day 2: Now that the countdown is on, every moment is precious with my furry friend. I cancel everything I can and spend time with Gannet sitting on my lap. She accepts the healing I offer her and seems relaxed.

Day 3: It is as if now that I have accepted that she is going to die soon, she seems more comfortable. I had not realised that my holding on to her was putting such pressure on her.

Day 4 and 5: We continue with the sitting, the healing and the good quality food. A measure of acceptance comes to me through having this time to say goodbye.

Day 6: I have to get real today. Although it is January, I go into the cold garden and start digging her grave. Even though it is a dull day, I wear my sunglasses to cover my tears. She has spent the last eighteen years in this garden and this is where her bones will lie. I know her spirit will fly free.

Day 7: I get a nice shoebox for her coffin and buy a pale pink fleece blanket to line it with. I pin an angel brooch to the blanket to watch over my pud in spirit. I am in bits but we

sit together and do the healing. She nibbles on the rich food.
Day 8: Transition essence (from Green Hope Farm) for both
her and me. Grief and Loss remedy (also from Green Hope
Farm) for me. Rescue Remedy for both of us, too. I tell her it
is okay to go. I sleep on the floor beside her to make sure she
is okay during the night.
Day 9: Nearly there now. Each moment has weight in the
context. I tell her that it is okay for her to go, and that if she
needs help from the vet we will do that. I tell her that I will
be with her all the time. She purrs.
Day 10: My heart is heavy. Is she still alive? I wake up
beside her and yes, still there.

Six months later, on the day of the summer solstice, Denis
the vet comes to help Gannet over the Rainbow Bridge.
Neither he nor I can believe that she lived an extra six
months with no drip, no kidney medication and high-
protein food that is not recommended for an animal with
kidney failure. He can't explain it. I am grateful for the extra
time with my furry friend. All I can think is that the good
organic food and the healing must have sustained her. Of
course I am distraught when she goes. Even though we
know something is going to happen you can never really be
prepared.
Looking back now, I can see with the benefit of hindsight
that I should have let her go long before I did. But I held on
too tightly. If I was to do it again, I would hope to have the
strength to let her go sooner. I now know that I was keeping

her alive for my emotional comfort rather than having her wellbeing as the top priority. My beloved father had passed away six months earlier and I simply could not cope with losing Gan as well. The healing energy contributed to keeping her alive - but I now believe it was the wrong thing to do.

It took me a long time to forgive myself for this, but I have. Through this experience I learned how to forgive myself, and how to be more compassionate with myself.

I know that however flawed, I was doing the best I could at the time. She was my best teacher, and I have taken on board all she taught me, and try to be a better Cat Mammy now. It is all I can do. It is all any of us can do - learn from our mistakes and resolve to do better from now on.

I understand now that if I accept what is happening instead of resisting and trying to control the uncontrollable, life flows more freely all round and death is easier to accept. The experience also taught me compassion for other pet guardians going through a similar situation, and this has helped me when I am doing healing with terminally ill animals and their guardians. I accept that people are doing the best they can. I offer my perspective and advice if I am asked, and support the guardian and the animal any way I can.

My best friend and teacher for eighteen years is at rest. Each summer I scatter rose petals on her grave marker at the bottom of the garden. We continue to be connected by the bond of love and I know we will be reunited in spirit one day.

Grieving your loss

Having your pet euthanized is traumatic for you. How could it be any other way? It is best to accept and acknowledge that trauma as real and valid. It is wise to accept that you will need to grieve for your beloved one just as you would for a human friend.

That process of grieving takes as long as it takes. I suggest that you give yourself as much time as you need. I suggest that you make no pronouncements like "I'll never get another cat/dog," or immediately rush to fill the void with a new pet. I worked in an animal sanctuary years ago and a woman came in looking for a black cat. During the course of the conversation, it transpired that her beloved black cat had died the previous week. She picked out a black cat that looked similar to her previous cat, stroked him, and picked him up. He bit her. He could feel her intense grief and stress and reacted to it. He was a different cat, as each animal is an individual. So rushing to get a new pet never works because we are trying to use the new pet to avoid feeling the pain and loss. As a clinical hypnotherapist for the last twenty years, I can tell you that trying to avoid emotional pain does not work. It just goes underground and will pop up again when you least expect it.

I suggest that you be gentle with yourself and your heart after your pet goes into spirit. Be kind to yourself. Don't rush into big decisions. Take your time and grieve your great loss. Acknowledging your grief is a way of honouring the great love you shared. As Buddhist teacher Jack Kornfield says, "Part of the art of quieting yourself is also to honour the tears that you carry."

Key Points

- It helps your pet if you stay calm and grounded during a crisis, whether that is an accident or a terminal diagnosis.

- Sometimes animals can live longer than originally predicted, with a good quality of life.

- If you lose a pet, be kind to yourself and give yourself as long as needed to grieve the loss, just as you would for a beloved human friend.

Chapter 8

Self Care is Vital

The quieter you become
The more you can hear

Baba Ram Dass

I know someone who trained as a healer but thought self-care was for sissies. They asked me for advice when they started getting burnt out and then ignored the advice. They had a nervous breakdown.

Special note to animal rescue workers and volunteers

I have done paid work in an animal sanctuary, and been a volunteer healer in another animal sanctuary for ten years. I have seen workers and volunteers eat, smoke and drink themselves into bad health because they have not taken account of the emotional toll of the work.

It takes a lot out of you to see the way animals are treated so badly. I have seen people burn out and break down. It is completely understandable. Think of it this way: you are doing this work because you love animals. You are working with animals that have been abandoned, abused or tortured. If you were working with humans who had been abandoned, abused or tortured you would not be allowed continue your work *unless* you received on-going support or therapy. There is no such rule when you are working with animals so you need to impose it on yourself. If you burn out or break down, you won't be able to help, and the animals need your help. So self-care is the foundation of being able to help the rescued animals.

You need to acknowledge the emotions, and find support from a friend or therapist if necessary. You need to create and maintain clear and healthy boundaries, and give yourself permission to say no. You need to find a way to switch off so that you get sufficient rest and recharge your batteries if you are to continue doing the work in the long term. (See the Resources section for ideas for self-support.) I strongly suggest that you need to connect with whatever you perceive to be your Higher Power, Higher Self, God or angels, and hand over or surrender the things you cannot do. At the end of a day when I feel guilty about not getting something done for a rescue animal, I say to my guardian angel: "Please take care of all the things I cannot do, mend, fix or control. Bless all the animals and help them in all possible ways."

Basic self care

Grounding

Grounding is key for self-care. Grounding means being consciously connected to the earth. It is very simple and easy to do and is beyond important. It is vital.

Years ago in Ireland all churches were built with very high steeples that had a metal cross on top. During a storm, lightning would hit the cross. A strip of metal conducted the lightning-energy safely down into the earth and kept the church intact. In other words, it grounded it. We are dealing with the same type of energy with healing. We need to respect it. There are many different ways to clear your energy field and renew your life-force energy. You do not have to use all of the methods I describe. However, it is important to use at least one of them. You can combine different ones. I suggest you experiment and find out what is right for you, and then use it on an on-going basis. To recap, here are two methods of grounding:

Method 1

Imagine the roots of a wise old tree growing from your root chakra down through the legs, through the soles of your feet down deep into the earth, connecting you with the earth. Be present in the present moment for yourself and therefore for your animal.

Method 2

Imagine there is a grounding cord going from your root chakra down into the centre of the earth. Expand this cord to the width of your body. Imagine it connects with blue healing light at the centre of the earth and that healing energy comes back up from it, filling your feet, legs, knees and root chakra the base of the spine, between the legs. Imagine this is a continuous circuit of supportive, healing energy for you. Set it on a timer to Automatic, Constant, and 100%.

The highly sensitive person

If you are reading this book, it is likely that you are a sensitive person. The Canadian psychotherapist Elaine Aron has written an excellent book called *The Highly Sensitive Person*, which she believes pertains to c.20% of the world population. The essence of it is that highly sensitive people process the world in a different way. It may be worth your while reading about this subject if you have a tendency to become overwhelmed by sensory input such as loud noises, too much interaction with others, lack of food or rest, or intense emotional experiences.

Turn off the tap

Make sure that you have turned off the universal healing tap when you have finished healing. Wash your hands, and imagine your energy coming back to you and the pet's energy going back to them. Rest.

Hydration and food

Drink 6-8 glasses of water over 24 hours to flush out your system.
If you are not already vegetarian, consider going veggie or vegan even one day a week. It will help your digestive system, your energy body, animals and the planet. As Marianne Williamson says, "Eating nutritious food supports you in living lightly and energetically within the body. In taking care of the body, you take better care of the spirit."

Epsom salts or sea salt

Sometimes if I have become very tired I have a shower after healing work. You can put Epsom salts or sea salt on a sponge or glove to use in the shower. A bath with Epsom/sea salt in it works very well to clear the aura.

Nature

Every blade of grass has its angel that bends over it and whispers 'Grow, Grow.' The Talmud

It clears the energy body to spend time in nature. Make sure you are present if you are walking in the park or by the sea. Bring your awareness behind your eyes and when your mind wanders, just return to that area behind the eyes. Let go of the need to reprimand yourself for losing focus. Your ability to be present in the present moment will grow like a muscle.

Meditation or mindfulness

Meditation or mindfulness is a great way to clear your energy field. It can be as easy as you allow it to be. Simply turn off the phone, sit still, and focus on breathing in and breathing out. As you do so, saliva may enter your mouth as the relaxation response is naturally triggered. A daily practice of even five or ten minutes is more useful than a practice once a week or at a weekend retreat. The reason for this is that it takes 16-30 repetitions to create a new habit. This process takes place through your actions creating a muscle memory and the plasticity of neuronal connections. Neurons (brain cells) that fire together, wire together through repetitive action. They create the new habit of mindfulness or meditation. In the Resources section you will see suggestions for Mindfulness books and CDs or downloads.

Self-healing practice

Get into the habit of doing energy healing on yourself every day, even for five or ten minutes. Here are the simple instructions again:

Close your eyes and take three calming deep breaths to centre yourself. Imagine that Cosmic or Christ energy (or God energy, Earth Healing Grid energy or whatever you wish to call it) is coming down from the Universe and in through the crown of your head. It comes to your neck and branches out down the arms and out through your hands. Hold your hands on your lap, facing each other. Let the cosmic energy flow into them and create a ball of white light between your hands. Let it build up for about five minutes. Direct this energy into yourself for at least five minutes.

Sound healing

Use Solfeggio tones from YouTube.com or a CD/download to balance your energy field through the vibration of sound healing.

Tuning fork: Use a tuning fork of 528 hertz which is the vibration of unconditional love. The sound of the fork vibrations clears stress from your aura.

Advanced self care

Run your energy

Turn off the phone and sit still. Breathe. Smile to raise your vibration. (It's not life-threatening, it's just meditation!) Check your grounding. Imagine your grounding cord and widen it to the width of your body. Imagine it connects with the centre of the earth and that healing energy comes back up from it, filling your feet, legs, knees and root chakra at the base of the spine, between the legs. Imagine this is a continuous circuit of supportive, healing energy for you. Set it on a timer to Automatic, Constant, and 100%.

Now imagine a white light coming down, bringing Cosmic/Universal/Christ light with it. Call it by whatever name is right for you. The light comes in to the crown chakra, down the back; it turns at the root chakra, goes up the front of the body, up through the crown and out into the energy field. It also goes out through the arms and hands into the energy field. The energy field is connected in to the grounding cord so that any foreign energy is immediately and automatically grounded into the earth where it is safely recycled. Imagine this is a continuous circuit of supportive, healing energy for you. Set it on a timer to Automatic, Constant, and 100%.

Run both the grounding circuit and the cosmic energy circuit in the background. Renew them once every 24 hours.

Permission rose

Imagine a beautiful rose in front of your solar plexus. Your

solar plexus is your power centre. This rose is a Permission Rose. Put it in place once a day in the morning. It gives you permission to be as you are, and other people permission to be as they are. It helps free you up from the drama of trying to control other people. You can only control yourself. You may be able to influence others but people are going to do what they are going to do - or not.

Focus your attention and energy on your own life and let others go their own way. I am including this in an animal healing book because we inevitably have to interact with other humans (even though many Animal People would prefer to interact only with animals!)

Visualisation: Imagine a white light clearing your energy

field and taking any foreign energy <u>outside your aura</u> and blowing it up so that it is recycled or repurposed into something safe and useful.

Clearing your chakras visualisation

It is easy to download a free sound recorder app onto your phone and record the following. Listening to the sound of your own voice is a powerful way to relax. If you choose to do this, do not listen to the audio when you are driving as you can lose focus and cause an accident.

Turn off alarms and notifications and sit still. Breathe. Smile to raise your vibration. Check that you are grounded and have a grounding cord the width of your body connected with the centre of the earth. Breathe in deep relaxation and breathe out tension. Imagine a white light coming down through your crown chakra and flowing down to your root chakra. It turns red and as it does, any foreign energy is released into your grounding cord. Breathe in deep relaxation and breathe out tension. Your root chakra easily balances itself now given the chance. Repeat silently to yourself: I am safe, secure and supported.

Focus now on your sacral chakra. The white light turns a beautiful orange and as it does, any foreign energy is released into your grounding cord. Repeat silently to yourself: I am connected to others in a healthy way. My life is sweet.

Focus now on your solar plexus. The white light turns

yellow, and as it does, any foreign energy is released into your grounding cord. Repeat silently to yourself: I am confident and I act with power and compassion.

Focus now on your heart chakra. The white light turns pale pink and green, and as it does, any foreign energy is released into your grounding cord. Repeat silently to yourself: In a healthy way, I am loving and I am loved.

Focus now on your throat chakra. The white light turns turquoise, and as it does, any foreign energy is released into your grounding cord. Repeat silently to yourself: I express my soul purpose now.

Focus now on your third eye chakra between your eyes. The white light turns indigo, and as it does, any foreign energy is released into your grounding cord. Repeat silently to yourself: My intuition grows stronger and clearer every day now.

Focus now on your crown chakra at the top of your head. The white light turns violet, and as it does, any foreign energy is released into your grounding cord. Repeat silently to yourself: I am connected to my divine self.

In your own time, open your eyes and come back fully to the place where you are, feeling relaxed and refreshed.

Key Points

- If you want to offer on-going energy healing to your pet, you must commit to self-care.

- If you are an animal rescue worker or volunteer, it is even more important.

- Choose and implement some of the listed options for self-care on a daily, on-going basis.

Chapter 9

Creating Conditions for Good Health

Happiness is the highest form of health.

Dalai Lama

What your animal needs for good health

The single thing that will make your animal the happiest is to have your undivided peaceful attention, where she is not competing against the phone, the tablet, the computer or the television. Make time to sit quietly in love and gratitude with your pet. Or play with them when they feel playful. Roll around the floor with them and enjoy the moment. They will be delighted. After they have passed into spirit, you will be glad. Because these are the times you will remember.

Physical

Once the basics of food, water, shelter, fresh air and exercise have been covered, here are some suggestions that may improve the quality of your pet's life.

Food quality

If you had an amazing car that was a thing of beauty, which ran on unleaded petrol, you wouldn't put diesel into it and expect it to continue to work. Yet that is what we do with our own bodies and the bodies of our animals. As humans, we have polluted and degraded our beautiful earth that gives us food. Apart from being an animal healer, I have also been a pet sitter and dog walker for about twelve years, as animals are my passion. In the past six years, I couldn't tell you the amount of animals I have seen that needed to be changed on to sensitive or hypoallergenic diets. The symptoms prompting these changes have been rashes, loss of appetite, diarrhoea and weight loss. The new diets are mostly either wheat or grain free and therefore gluten free. The animals have mostly responded with improved health. When you think about what dogs or cats eat in the wild, they would not naturally eat cereals or grain unless it was in the stomach of their prey.

Getting the food right is key. A homeopathic vet I know recommends raw food for all her animal clients. Some animals may not eat it though so it doesn't work for everyone. My suggestion is that you provide either a raw diet or the best quality high protein grain-free (or at least gluten free) diet with both wet and dry food that you can for your cat or dog. Gluten is thought to have an inflammatory effect on the bowel, and provides food for viruses and bacteria to feed on. Naturally if your animal has a medical condition you need to take on board the advice of your vet and act accordingly.

Water

Another thing we humans have polluted is water. Even tap water has chlorine in it, so strong that you might even be able to smell it. Your pet certainly can smell it - that is why they would prefer to drink rainwater from a muddy pool as opposed to tap water. Now, using bottled water is not a viable option for planet earth with the way it degrades into micro beads and pollutes the food chain from plankton to whales. Plastic water jug filters are not biodegradable either. A sustainable option that I can vouch for is Prill Beads. You buy them once, for about €20, and they last forever. Amazing. I have been using the same bag of beads for eight years now. I drink the water it filters and so do my pets. See the Resources section for details.

Access to nature

All animals need access to fresh air and nature for their well-being. A cat, for instance, needs contact with the earth, grass and safe green plants in order to feel peaceful. If your cat is an indoor cat, and you have access to a garden, consider creating even a small catio where she can have access to fresh air and nature. If possible, put different levels in it so your cat can jump up.

If this is not possible, then enrich your pet's indoor area with safe plants (e.g. don't use lilies as every part of them are toxic to cats) and grass, and a tray of earth which is to give her contact with the earth, not for use as a litter tray. (Hopefully she will have got the memo about that!) Plants can be grouped together to create a small oasis for your cat.

Sense of smell

Bleach, the chemicals in scented candles, plug-in air fresheners, aerosol air fresheners, spray bottle air fresheners and second-hand fumes from smoking or vaping all create a toxic load on your pet's liver. Please avoid them where possible.

Coping with change

Your animal loves you. Presumably you love your animal or you wouldn't be reading this book. In order to feel safe, your pet needs stability and routine. Most pets hate change so when change inevitably happens, they need more attention than usual to help them feel secure. Many pets have the emotional range of at least a three year old child (or more) so think about the things you would do to help a child feel safe and secure.

One of the small things that can help is to use Rescue Remedy. The purpose of this flower essence is to calm, comfort and reassure. (I should have shares in the company because I have used so much of it over the years!) If you are going to use it I suggest that you buy the pet or children's alcohol-free version. If you can't get that, then use the ordinary version which has alcohol in it, but use it on the back of the neck on older animals or animals with kidney/liver problems. It is absorbed into the energy field from the back of the neck.

In a time of transition, offering extra energy healing helps your pet cope better with change. Your pet benefits from the healing and you benefit by having to sit down whether or not you feel you have time!

Play

Another way to help your pet feel safe is to play with him/her. In the animal world, play is a form of communication and bonding. Your pet wants your undivided attention so turn off phones and tablets while playing. It will enrich both their lives and yours to play every day.

If your cat is indoors or recuperating from an illness, try putting on cat videos from www.youtube.com. Put in the search term "videos for cats to watch" as otherwise you will get ten million videos of cats being funny! Some of my cats love them and some ignore them.

Leading the way

You and your pet are a unit. Your pet is very sensitive and tuned in to your emotional state. Therefore if you are stressed, your pet will be stressed. If you are calm and peaceful, your pet will be too. You set the emotional tone for your pet. When cats are stressed, for instance, they often pee outside the litter tray. They may be stressed for a number of reasons such as a new house, a new cat in their territory or a scare they got. But sometimes they are stressed because they are picking up your stress and tension. Therefore anything you can do to reduce your stress and let it go will also help your pet. Many times I have seen an animal get exactly the same type of disease as their guardian, because they are trying to help by taking on the illness. We are all connected. Looking after yourself well helps your pet too.

Say only kind words

In his book, The Hidden Messages in Water, Dr Masaru Emoto describes his discovery that crystals formed in frozen water reveal changes when specific, concentrated thoughts are directed toward them. Since we and our animals consist of 70% water, this finding is relevant to us. The essence of his work is that kind words produce harmonic water crystal shapes and vibrations. Derogatory, unkind, shaming or cruel words produce malformed water crystal shapes and vibrations. So please be careful what you say to your pet. And indeed yourself and other people too.

Dr Masaru found that using the affirmation "Love and thanks" over food (especially microwaved food) created more harmonic crystal shapes. You can repeat "Love and thanks" three times over the animal, its food and its water bowl too. Three repetitions raise the vibrational energy. It is especially good to use this phrase if you have to microwave food for your pet, as the microwaving process deforms the energy field of the food. If you can, it is better to heat food for your pet in a saucepan on a stove or cooker top.

Energy wise

To reduce the amount of dissonant electromagnetic field (EMF) energy bombarding your pet, plug out the broadband or Wi-Fi connection at night. Move their bed away from plugged in electrical devices. Generally speaking, cats like electromagnetic energy waves and that is why you will find them lying on your laptop! Dogs are the opposite and they can find them very stressful. One dog I did healing on improved hugely when his guardian moved his bed away from the broadband transmitter in his home. His anxiety level reduced noticeably and he stayed a lot calmer.

Another option is to use Green Hope Farm Flower Essence Golden Armour. It protects your animal's energy field and therefore strengthens its immune system. Green Hope Farm has a catalogue of Animal Wellness flower remedies. The details are listed in the Resources section.

Bach Flower Remedies for Animals are another useful tool to help create emotional and energetic balance in your pet. Investigate which Bach Flower remedy most closely fits the profile of your pet and use that.

Sound healing

Go to YouTube.com and type in Solfeggio healing for animals and try out some sound healing for your pet. Observe them as they listen to the sounds; if they like it, fine, if not, turn it off. There is also music for cats and music for dogs.

Key Points

- Review your pet's food and water so that it is of the best possible quality.

- Ensure your pet has access to nature.

- Reduce the toxic load on the liver of your pet.

- Be your pet's emotional leader by being calm.

- Reduce the amount of EMF waves affecting your pet.

Chapter 10

Other Healing Resources for Your Pet

No matter what the situation, remind yourself - I have a choice.
Deepak Chopra

Complementary therapy options

Energy healing is a wonderful tool to help your animal, but there is no single therapy or approach that works for every animal and every condition. In this chapter I share some of the options that I have explored for animals in my care over the years.

Wrap up

Case history of a hyperactive dog

I was asked to do some work on a dog called Sandy, who was very anxious and hyperactive. I gave her some healing, and also suggested that a Thundershirt might help her. To check if it might, we put a T shirt on her, tying it up around the waist. The effect was dramatic. She calmed down immediately. The idea comes from the practice of swaddling babies to calm them down, or using a weighted duvet to help people with autism feel calmer and safer as it reduces over-stimulation. There are now Thundershirts for cats too. You could try a snug fitting cat or dog coat first to see if it would help. They are said to improve the situation for 80% of animals. Karmawrap is a similar product. https://www.thunderworks.com/

The Emotion Code

The Emotion Code is a very simple and effective form of energy healing, designed to correct imbalances in the body and energy field. Once the imbalances are corrected, it allows the body and energy field to heal itself, as it is designed to do. It was created by Dr Bradley Nelson, an American chiropractor. It works on people and animals. Dr Nelson believes that the most common underlying imbalance is trapped emotions. The premise is that a trapped emotion consists of energy which can either cause or contribute to a physical symptom and/or a behavioural issue. It does this by distorting the energy field. You use a chart to identify which emotion it is of the sixty on the chart. You identify this by muscle testing, which is very simple and easy. Then you focus on that emotion while running a magnet from the animal's nose to the base of their spine, either three or ten times. The trapped emotion has a particular energy signature which is released by the action of the magnet on the governing meridian, which runs from the top of the upper lip in humans to the base of the spine, and from the nose to the base of the spine in animals.

Dr Nelson found that once released, the emotion did not recur. Please note that I have found that sometimes the results are immediate and dramatic. Sometimes they take a few days and are more subtle. Sometimes a few sessions are needed. For example, I might release anxiety from a dog, and it appears to come back. What is actually happening is that the first layer of anxiety was released, and then the second layer comes up to be released and so on. All of the information needed to use the Emotion Code, including muscle testing, is contained in the book of the title and on Dr Nelson's website as listed below.

- Dr Bradley Nelson's website is www.discoverhealing.com
- The Emotion Code book - revised and updated edition published in 2019.
- The Emotion Code chart of trapped emotions https://discoverhealing.com/emotion-code-chart-guide/
- Free video on how to do muscle testing on his website https://discoverhealing.com/your-guide-to-muscle-testing/

Case history of spraying cat

A cat called Vernon began spraying in the house when he felt threatened by a new cat in the neighbourhood. I tuned in to him to offer him distant healing. He agreed to the healing. I identified the trapped emotions by the process described and cleared them by running a magnet from nose to tail of an imaginary Vernon sitting on my knee. Then I worked on his companion cat in the same way. The spraying stopped. It restarted a week later after an incident between Vernon and the new cat. I did another session of distant emotion code healing and also suggested that Kalms tablets might help Vernon relax. At the time of writing, the spraying has not restarted.

How to know if your animal is sick

Guide by Dr Andrew Jones: Dog and Cat Health Secrets. See www. drjonesnaturalpet.com

Things to ask your holistic vet about

I have brought many rescue animals for both conventional and complementary therapy vet treatments over the last ten years. Some therapies have worked for some animals, other therapies on other animals. There is no one "Magic Bullet" therapy that works every time for every animal. When conventional treatment is yielding no results, I suggest that along with regular energy healing, you investigate the following with a holistic vet:

- Acupuncture
- CBD oil as an anti-inflammatory and pain reliever
- Chiropractic
- Herbs
- Homeopathy, including remedies for before euthanasia, such as Arsenicum Album 30C.
- Low level light therapy for joint pain
- Raw food diet

Homeopathy case history

One of my cats, Sid, was very ill some time ago. He had bloody diarrhoea and was vomiting. I took him to the conventional vet who prescribed antibiotics which had no effect. I took him back and he was put on a drip for twenty four hours, with new antibiotics. Still no effect. I offered him healing but he was very restless and agitated and said no. He wanted to get outside and although I normally would keep a sick cat inside for supervision, I let him out into the garden. He lay on a patch of bare earth, even in the rain. He was tapping in to the healing frequency of the earth.

It was, of course, a bank holiday weekend. (There seems to be a law in the cat world that if you are going to get sick, do it after the vet has closed or on a bank holiday weekend.) The next day, in desperation, I emailed a homeopathic vet who suggested Merc Cor and Kali Bich homeopathic remedies. I had the Kali Bich and I gave him several doses as directed. He seemed no better for a few hours, but the next morning, he was looking for food for the first time in a week. Thankfully he made a full recovery after that.

Other options to investigate

- Tellington T Touch - some of the movements are especially good for calming animals, changing difficult behavioural patterns and improving immune system function.

- Kalms for anxiety in dogs and cats - main ingredient is l-trypophan, a precursor of serotonin, the feel good hormone.

- Protocol for a cat with Irritable Bowel Syndrome.
  See www.naturalcatcareblog.com (I used this for a 22 year old cat in the sanctuary and it helped.)

- Natural remedy information from vet Dr Andrew Jones: www.drjonesnaturalpet.com and also on his youtube.com channel which is called "Veterinary Secrets."

- Diatomaceous earth for parasite control - I have successfully used this for my feral cat. See the video on Dr Jones's channel for dosage and usage.

- Water Filter: Effective, cheap, environmentally friendly and long-lasting water filter: Prill Beads
  https://magicofmagnesium.weebly.com/precious-prills.html

- Low level light therapy for joint problems and pain
  https://animalwellnessmagazine.com/light-therapy-for-dogs-and-cats/

- Alternative therapy information https://www.whole-dog-journal.com/

- Information on goats http://goodgoats.blogspot.com/

- Dr Gloria Dodd Holistic vet information
  https://www.everglonaturalvet.com/

Flower remedies

- Greenhope Farm Flower Essences have an Animal Wellness catalogue. https://www.greenhopeessences.com/
- Bach Flower Remedies: Find the remedy that most closely fits the profile of your pet and use that. Here is one website to explore: https://www.bachfloweradvice.co.uk/bach-flowers-and-animals

Vaccines

If your animal is sick, do not get them vaccinated until they are better. In fact, research information as to whether regular vaccination is right for your animal. See this link for information on homeopathic alternatives to vaccines so that you can make an informed decision. https://holisticanimalremedies.com/

Vegetarian dog treats

Check out Woofstuff.ie for vegetarian dog treats, which are especially good for animals with sensitive stomachs

Resources for recharging your own batteries

Williams, Mark & Penman, Danny. *Mindfulness: A practical guide to finding peace in a frantic world* book and CD. Little, Brown. 2011
App based on the book
http://franticworld.com/mindfulness-apps/
Hickey, Marese. *How to Love Yourself in Less than 50 Years.* Createspace. 2016.
Calm app from Google Play costs €50 a year
Aron, Elaine. *The Highly Sensitive Person: How to Survive and Thrive When the World Overwhelms You.* Harper Collins. 2017.
Donna Eden Energy Medicine: See youtube.com
5 minute daily routine https://youtu.be/gffKhttrRw4
How to do self-havening for self-healing See youtube.com
https://youtu.be/ILhPOKTTkAY
Go to youtube.com and type in Jason Stephenson meditations for free guided healing meditations

Holistic vets in Ireland

Emily McAteer, Portmarnock, Co. Dublin
www.holisticvetdublin.com
Emily is a homeopathic vet, and also has another vet in her practice who does herbs and acupuncture. Highly recommended.
Tom Farrington, West Cork. A homeopathic vet who will send remedies by post. Email: farrington.vet@gmail.com
Gary Creegan in Lissenhall Vets, Swords, Co. Dublin does acupuncture. www.lissenhallvet.ie

Animal chiropractor

Ted McLaughlin chiropractor https://www.equine-performance.com/practitioner.htm

Further reading

Emoto, Dr Masaru. *The Hidden Messages in Water*. Atria. 2005.
Nelson, Dr Bradley. *The Emotion Code*. Vermillion, 2019.
Pellegrino-Estrich, Robert. *The Power to Heal.* Brazil: Self printed by Pellegrino-Estrich, Robert. 2008.
Shine, Betty. Mind Magic; *The Key to the Universe*. Corgi. 1992
Stein, Diane. *The Natural Remedy Book for Dogs and Cats*. Crossing Press.1994.
Stein, Diane. *Natural Healing for Dogs and Cats*. Crossing Press.1993.
Tellington-Jones, Linda. *The Tellington TTouch*. Penguin. 1999

Request from the author

Thank you very much for reading this book. I hope you have enjoyed it. As a self-published author, I have no marketing budget. So if you feel that animals would benefit from energy healing, I would really appreciate if you could share information about the book on your social media and also take the time to put an honest review of it on Amazon.com, Amazon.co.uk or Amazon.au
Thanks for your help.

Contact

www.maresehickey.com
Facebook @PetandPeopleHealer
Twitter @maresehickey1
Instagram Marese Hickey

Additional Healing Tips for Readers

I am offering a short Tip sheet with extra ideas for animal healing that I use regularly and to good effect. Also included are more ideas for Self Care. If you would like to receive this in exchange for your email address (which will be respected and not shared with anyone else) please go to www.maresehickey.com Use the Contact Form and write "Tip Sheet" in the comment box.

Praise for author

The Tale of Harry Three Paws

A Purrfect Gift

Such a beautiful little cat story, with an important message about how cats like to be cared for, how they hope and dream, just as we do, and how they love to heal us with their loving purr. The author wrote this as a childrens' book, and I think children will love it and find it easy to read. It is beautifully written, from the cat's point of view, and very moving. It would make a perfect gift for a child who wants to own a cat. THE TALE OF HARRY THREE PAWS is good for adults too, so it is a rare 'crossover book'. I enjoyed the spiritual aspect of it, always something to smile about, full of hope and light, with glimpses into the heaven world. It's written with sensitivity, clarity and warmth. I hope lots of people discover this delightful book. I shall treasure my copy.

Elaine Clover on Amazon

Letting Go of the Past: Simple and Fast Energy Healing for Limiting Beliefs and Minor Childhood Trauma

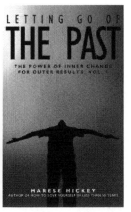

Well worth reading. The author discusses the benefits of using the Tapas Acupressure Therapy (TAT) for healing old beliefs and childhood trauma. She explains how energy clots can be accumulated in the meridians etc. of the body and why it is necessary to release these blockages to allow for healing.

Amazon Customer, Australia

5 Stars

An absorbing read which fosters healing in a way that is powerful and natural

I am so delighted to have discovered Marese's books. They are such absorbing reads, imbued with a gentle healing power that subtly seeps into your being as you go. Marese helps you connect to yourself, fostering healing in a way that is totally effortless and natural. I guess letting go is never "easy" but this great little book certainly does help!

Pamela C

How to Love Yourself in Less Than 50 Years: Move from Low Self-esteem to Self-Compassion and Energise Your Life, Soul and Spirit

I gave this book 5 stars because it has been written by a lovely human being who has inspired me to be the best that I can be. It obviously has been written from the heart in a very easy and articulate way and will resonate with all those who are on a soul journey. Admiration and gratitude for sharing these lovely words.

Michelle McLouglin, Amazon USA

Index

Printed in Poland
by Amazon Fulfillment
Poland Sp. z o.o., Wrocław

60371276R00074